ABSTRACT
CORES

To Amy,
Best luck
thanks for supporting
these early efforts

KIM WEBB

Special thanks for editorial support: Miriam Jones
                                         VieVee
                                         Perri Giavannucci
                                         Renee Tambeau

And massive technical assitance: Tim Suliman

Published by The Ridgeway Press
              P.O. Box 120
              Roseville, MI 48066

Publisher: M.L. Liebler

This book is dedicated to the Naugal Julian who was reported to be a hopeless libertine, and those of us that chase our freedom through a poem. GOD SPEED.

ABSTRACT CORES

The Table of Contents:

OUTLOUD

INLOUD

OUTLOUD

THE WALK

The Bodhisattva's eyes
and Renior's barmaid
are whispering between
each other as we walk
The night is solid
as a pillar
pulled over into these
Cossack fragments
ruined little details
that stood like CITIES
when we were stronger

A message rises up
from a crack in the walk:
"Unlock the stone hearts of the trees"
they are pumping this
organic geometry
that feels like music
and underscores the
secret places between
PATHOS and EROS
a place outside this
junkyard of names
that undid your dress
It's not just safe
decadence out there
there is nothing to be
decadent against
when you unlock
the stone hearts
of those trees
you are both vulnerable
and invincible
in the same pulse of light ...
the entire universe

is an agreement
that grants your being presence

The Bodhisattva's eyes
and Renior's barmaid
are whispering between
each other as we walk
The night is solid
as a pillar
pulled over into these
Cossack fragments
ruined little details
that stood like CITJES
when we were stronger   # # #

UIS-A-UIS

The sky is an Aquamarine. It is not like an Aquamarine, everything else in this story is like something else ... but not the sky. The sky is a hard, cool, pale blue Aquamarine; it is set in gold along the horizon. The people of Vis-A-Vis seem bent on staring off to that horizon, but never up, never down, and never ever at each other. It is an odd place, the town of Vis-A-Vis, its very name a paradox. It sits under the shores of the deepest, blackest lake to ever stop the light and not give it back. There is only one way into Vis-A-Vis and that is through the lake, neither across nor around ... through the lake. That is how I came to be here. It was a lovely summer day and I dove from a high precipice in my cut-off blue jeans into its black embrasive stillness. The water was not water at all, but a vortex of earthy warm feminine laughter. It was no substance - all sound, and the velocity of my dive carried me at an even constant speed into the nothingness below. Because Black Lake is actually a pool of nothing, anything that happens to be something rushes back to the surface, but your body keeps falling. Thoughts, desires, feelings, ideas, sensations, images, and memory of all description race away from the body like little bubbles of air. The farther you fall the less of you there would seem to be, and yet you - a kind of essential you - do finally arrive in Vis-A-Vis. The you that arrives in Vis-A-Vis is not exactly the thing you always called you, but you are present. It's all very confusing I know. When I first arrived, I took one look at the sky, that Aquamarine sky, and wanted to be like it. So, I became the pavement of Vis-A-Vis. I was hard like the sky, just smaller and more opaque. I liked being pavement. I liked the rhythm of the town's movement playing against me. I would have probably been content to remain as pavement and stare up each day at that Aquamarine sky, but an event occurred which changed all of that.

Back above the lake, lived a magician and his wife. The magician's wife had grown despondent for reasons only she knew and had taken to long walks by the shores of Black Lake. The magician was not comfortable with his love straying so close to that blackness which never gave back so much as a reflection. The magician dazzled the woman, whose name was Arethusa, with remarkable feats and great courage. Yet, Arethusa was pulled ever more closely to the shores of Black Lake. A day finally came when she disrobed and leapt away from the banks into the nothingness below. Arethusa arrived at Vis-A-Vis and became a Holly Hock bush. She broke through me - the pavement - in one urgent burst of growth. I was broken into, no longer solid like the sky. The magician on finding Arethusa's clothes by the lake dove in after her. He ran up and down my streets in search of her. In one of my alleys, he discovered a Holly Hock bush and cut a huge stalk of blooms to give to Arethusa when he found her.

The sky is a hard, cool, pale blue Aquamarine. The pavement has been broken, something grew resplendently and got cut down the day the magician brought his "love" to town. Vis-A-Vis, Vis-A-Vis where you are often face to face with an altogether different sort of continuity.   ###

Excerpt from "BRIDGE BUILDING"

It's getting near dusk
and it's summer
early summer -

in the open field
away from stands of trees
that are already dark
fireflies set up a slow
mendicant rhythm-
it is still here
and quiet
the air carries different smells
pine and gardenia
the mossy organic
wet smell of water
and I am alone
and lying back
in the coolness
of the grass ...

The days are round
and I imagine your
sleepy eyes opening
gentle like lavender.

The nights brush
across the bed with
the delicacy of sable
and our energies become
taste and tonic.

When I am quiet
I hear the CRACKLE of campfire,
sometimes on a beach
other times in a forest.

There is an inescapable
bridge at twilight
that hums HIGH like ginseng or mint
other times it speaks slow >>>>
like wormwood or mistletoe
it beckons the traveler to cross
and there dreams walk erect
shadows take form
abstract fields of energy
are bathed in an inner glow.
We rest there in
a crystal of moments
whose hard geometry
accepts only some
transparent likeness -
an image reflected
along endless facets
whole and undivided
they multiply
and cover the landscape
like a single green
local and absolute.   # # #

THE JADED AND THE JUSTIFIED

The jaded and the justified
trade glances across the deceased.
It's a suspension of the obvious
and in that moment
we are I suppose
inclined to pick sides.
Am I jaded?
Am I justified?

The rhetorical postures
of reason
collide
perpetuating forever
the mask of the outlaw
and the mask of the lawman.

But who was the victim
and what was her name? ...
the body
the one slain.
Which of the four winds
could she call to her
as she dreamt
and do those dreams
as yet exist
outside the prescribed
script of reason?
The script that sends
the jaded out beyond the city limits
like a scout
and the justified
trailing behind
in endless pursuit.
It's always the same script
predictable as a 19TH Century landscape
with that large dark tree in the foreground

---

framing canvas center
where the eye can pretend
it's in some real space
and not a convention.
We believe the illusion.
Reason is a convention
not unlike that large dark tree
dividing splitting dividing
the world in TWO

me? I'm the protagonist
you the ole an-tagonist

could say we both agonist
AGONY
Where'd that body go?
Who was the victim
and what was her name
the body
the one slain?

The full voice of dark lakes
a green hum along the firmament
the heart of a bird racing like an orgasm
rise
RISE
wake that body up
buzz little buddy buzz
just wake up out of this fixation
and into the
dream.   # # #

VIVID

The waterbearer and an iconoclast
were drinking Ethiopian Haraar
beneath a thorny locust tree
that shaded a corner
of the patio
at Sloan Rainey's bungalow.
The morning air was still cool
and the coffee had the aroma
of a soupcon of cinnamon
that lifted on occasion
above a twisted floral mixture
from an obsessive container garden
that grounded the songs
from rather ordinary birds.
On the table next to the coffee
cups and saucers still dotted
with crumbs from English muffins
was the newspaper that landed
each morning with metropolitan
weight against the stone steps.

An iconoclast was staring at the unopened
mound of newsprint - it was
a scissor stare.
The waterbearer's head was tilted
back eyes closed.
Sloan Rainey lay dead in the middle
of the patio, a few buzzing insects
circling suspiciously not totally
convinced of their good fortune.

The waterbearer began to sing
an oddly melodic Middle Eastern
sounding chant. I recall each
of these details with lucid clarity

---

as if Sloan's passing made more
room in the present. The waterbearer, the
iconoclast and I were together for perhaps
the first time and none of us were talking.
On leaving our eyes each connected below
language and blood to some elemental spark
squeezed from a dark moment.

Later, I heard they pried a
crumpled piece of sketch pad from Sloan's
hand. He had written down:
    "It doesn't mean anything
    that it doesn't mean anything"
he skipped a space and then wrote the word
    "vivid."   # # #

BOURGY SUMMER
(spoken the way you'd imagine Carl Sandburg would tell a large tale)

It's a HOT summer day
by the pool. The whole place smells
of coconut chlorine and semen.
Even SUNglasses have a smell
on days such as this - it's a hot plastic smell
the smell of America with her pants down.
My poolside colleagues are an assem-blage
of products expensive products
none of which they have personally made
and none of which have known the time it takes
for the earth to circumnavigate
the sun
even once.

Enter Mau-reen.

Now Maureen
has
a body no man deserves to glimpse even darkly between the
Venetian blinds
of their own imaginations.
The only thing I ever saw that instilled greater lust was a left
handed Fender Strat ...
and I was afraid to touch that.
Maureen dove into the pool
the eyes of 10,000 expensive products followed her
with enough concentration to divide the molecules of water
from the molecules of chlorine -
thus sparing the lifeguard a water test. She lifted herself
to hot cement and
by the time a swiftly provided lounge
had accepted her into its arms she knew the combined
inventory of products by the pool. She is not as impressed as I.
I marvel at the speed of their delivery the sly order in which
they are presented even the carefully chosen baubles that lend

---

credence
to their actual existence.
Mau-reen dives into the pool a second time
and surfaces BY MY LEGS.

"Hi," she says.
"Hi," I say.
"I hear you are an artist." She lifts the word to a new level
of importance.
"Actually, I'm a 1966 Ford Galaxy 500 with Taoist sensibilities
and Jungian dreams."

- we pause -

"I always wanted someone to draw rne naked," was her reply.

Now a lesser artist would not have known WHEN to compromise
their work - we left 12 seconds later. I actually did manage
three drawings of which no slides exist. One can not be too
careful with historians behind every rock and tree. Historians
who are apt to draw conclusions instead of images. Conclusions
based on experience sans Maureen. Historians who have doubtfully
ever experienced head and ice cubes simultaneously nor could
they conceive of a four day barrage on your sexual stamina where
nothing is repeated and
nothing is left out.

Mau-reen left a lipstick message on my mirror, it read:
"PAINT THAT".

So much for the natural resource that wakes to find itself a
price tag. I will be the first to admit that I was bourgeoisie
BOUGHT and SOLD.   # # #

A THEORETICAL POEM

Art is an action
received as well as possible
inside a point of time.

Art is an action
received as well as possible
inside a point of time.

It was just the sunlight on a glass of iced tea in an ordinary
room.

Rooms without clothes
two voices
unabashed
and handsome
across the carpet.
A suspension of urgency
in a place as stifling
as this,
and in your flower
that sang against
a dusty weaver's loom
a bell rang out
from that catholic church
old as Jesus
and into the town.
The town literally had a square
and we danced there
and divided
roots and rooms
envisioned upon
some sad merchant's stand
and eventually
returned -

back again to the aforementioned glass of tea on ice, and the

---

sunlight on it.

We remembered past lives
earlier lives
and we returned to
them in our dreams.
Those dreams told us
how ordinary we were.
They showed how we
raked muck in stables,
ate bad potatoes,
and died of regular reasons
in pretty average beds.
But, then again,
we really didn't
buy into any of that shit.
So, we checked out the future.
It was this nebulous
cloudy substance,
and we felt really nervous
trusting ourselves with it -

but, there we were in an ordinary room ... and there was that
glass of iced tea, and it still had sunlight on it.

What were we
supposed to do after all?
I mean there was no sense
of urgency,
we weren't looking
for anything,
but we had to do something.
Now, why
we had to do something
I don't know;
but we did
and we knew it.
There was no
sense of urgency
but there was that
glass of iced tea,
and we both liked it.
We agreed it was good
and we looked at it
in an odd way.

We felt it stood for us
luminous
and beaded with sweat -
and I don't know why
I thought that
or what makes me
relive that minute
instead of just remembering it,
but I do.

Art is an action
received as well as possible
inside a point of time.　　# # #

"I'D RATHER BE JUNG THAN A JUNGIAN"
C. G. Jung

Walking to this artesian well for a drink, I meet a Cartesian wearing a Descartes button on the lapel of his leather jacket. It's about 95 degrees - I question the Descartes button. The Cartesian smiles and leads me to this bar, it's called THE GREEN BEETLE. It's a dangerous bar he tells me, so we walk in. In the far corner of the room are two identically passionate twins, they have their tongues down each other's throats. The tender of the bar is cleaning his nails with a switchblade knife. He spikes it unconsciously into the bar sticking straight up. He asks us what we'll have? The Cartesian logically orders whiskies STRAIGHT UP. I notice a photograph of my soul mate behind the bar. "It's a small world," I say the way Laurie Anderson would. The Cartesian notices I'm referring to the photograph and just repeats the words BLACK and WHITE over and over for about an hour. Two little girls maybe 7 years old come in the bar. They order beers and draw a Hop Scotch board on the floor with some chalk from the pool table. The phone rings. It's my soul mate. She asks me how I'm doing? Things are good I say, I'm drinking whiskey with a Cartesian... I miss you. One of the 7 year old girls pulls out a .44 magnum and blows her friend away. The other girl falls down, gets up, and tells me: "It's o.k., I believe in cartoons."

DREAM SHIFT   (spoken while moving the index finger quickly between the lips)

O.K., I'm in Paris now with Pierre Bonnard. Everybody knows Pierre Bonnard had an overBEARING wife. She's there too, I've never been to Paris ... I take a look around. It seems it's smoggy in summer. Bonnard's wife doesn't have a name, that's history for you. She's speaking French (naturally) so I have no entry into their conversation except by gesture. She seems o.k. to me despite the rumors. I ask if I can take a bath... seems like the thing to do at the Bonnards.

DREAM SHIFT   (spoken while moving the index finger quickly between the lips)

I'm reading at this coffee house in Detroit. WOW, what a weird place to find oneself. What if my voice cracks? What if these little ditties have no mass appeal? What then? What if I just spoke to the fact that the future is ours to create? What if Detroit was better than Paris as the century turned? What if we were Bonnard, Picasso, Breton, DuChamp, Man Ray, Mallarme, Rimbaud,

Matisse, Jung and Freud? What if women had names here? That little girl back at the bar who drank beer and took the bullet? What did she know that I don't? Shit man, nothing seemed to stop her, and she was just playing HOP SCOTCH.   ###

DREAMING AWAKE

A field of pinwheels
    spinning.
A breeze to turn them.
Earth to anchor them.

Basil vinegarette
clean cotton

harmonica, drums, and cello

lip curved metal
hot strawberry tea

and I'm an anaconda
across your hips.

Drippy green vegetation
that humus smell
dry cracked hands
and broken nails.

Steamy pot bubbles
dinner smells
at sun down
and night just happens -
the paper boats
of kids
soaked along
the frog infested banks
of a willow time
creaking
the porch swing
to and fro.

A minor conversation

lunar and orange
in bare bulb light
quiet
and bound by porch railing
against the weight of night.

The darkness
we stare into
or divide by virtue
of bodies dreaming
out along the rocky
edges of these dirt roads
the birds watching
our movement
in a night
that could not ever
howl.   ###

THE KNOCK OF THE SPIRIT

I'm frightened
beyond the dark reflections
of trees in the puddles

on the earth heaved
sidewalks germane
to low rent districts

language and economics
speak low
and self aware

thunder rolls
and lightening
the token whining dog
keeps the unknown at bay

I feel you like
the smooth speed of a snake
on the first abstract trail
of my solitary choosing

the swift current
on whose surface
matter collides
and is torn
apart by terrain
to collide
and collide again

beyond the dark reflection
of trees
the edgy eyes
of a predator
knowing

by gentle expansions of the rib cage
your movement along the corridors
of an edifice
that appears solid
dealing its card
none-the-less
into the molten gathering
of a sun forgotten night   ###

VOICES

Bast is East
in full lunacy
I got a blanket of bones
I got some silver
and the essence of orchids
wrapped in incense sticks

goddess incarnate movin'
in a feline frame says
"You need some sky
in this world."
Her elder lesser emissary
had a pendant in the shape
of the sun that argued
with the silver it was made from
It was sweet actually -
sharing moon metal
and holding hands
the way centuries touch

and I couldn't tell you
I couldn't say for sure
but I thought I heard
this Old Kingdom voice
whispering up against
a membrane of time
that said
"Forgive us the pyramids
The Nile really ain't a river
it's more like a bathtub drain -
you ... you guys discovered that."

Bast and Anubis
were supposed to
have a date

---

and maybe they will this time
But that girl with
the sun made outta silver
so cool
so malleable
has got a voice that
sticks to me
like red clay when it rains
and I can't get it off
I can't get it off   # # #

IMPERSONAL DAWN

There is a green sovereign nation
buried under an age of concern
fractured and disordered
by the subtexts of attention

Rally your intent
and face an impersonal dawn

A sun unmoored
from a history
of stories
built from either / or
either I'm speaking in a coffeehouse
or an apartment
I'm speaking both in a coffeehouse
and an apartment - at this very moment
And in front of me
is a viscous liquid
stretching forward in time
illusory and tangible
to the same finger
during the same touch -
we all flow out here in odd moments
The whole opportunity gets
continually misread
because reason is so narrow
it misses more than it catches
and standing right next
to a sun catcher
is that sin tax collector

Yeah we go way back
we go back to a season ages ago
we go back to a season ages ago
when pain was present

---

in prism-colored smiles
and decisions were made ...
it was all either / or
and now those decisions
are laws that can't be broken
and walls so high
and your body is available
because you can't make it disappear
but the walls are so high
only a thief could get in
and the walls so high
and the walls so high
and the laws can't be broken
only a thief could get in
and history is repetitive
and stories are history
and either / or is one
kind of story

Rally your intent
and face an impersonal dawn

Rally your intent
and face an impersonal dawn

We can go out for a walk
like an echo away from its source
footsteps inside of footsteps
and still hold the vibration of sound
that lets candles and stars
burn against the same night sky
the audacity of a candle
burning against the stars
The walk through a grove
and the song rising through it
where a dumb bird
of total freedom
sings one time
it sings ONE time
and it is present here
in a grove going
in a spiral of
possibilities

Rally your intent

and face an impersonal dawn

Rally your intent
and face an impersonal dawn

Rally your intent
and face an impersonal dawn

There is an equivalency of detail
from which language rises
It's the number on the door
to your apartment
the garden fence
where you hung your dress
the inflection of a name
the handwriting on a
canceled check
and in tossing them
over the walls
the walls come down
and you're bare
devoid of the currency
of social containers
and you're not alone
and standing on the
shores of a black black lake
where the surface accepts
any flicker of flame
the stars are burning
the way stars are prone
and candles are burning
and all the light across
that surface is an agreement
and you're bare
and you're not alone

Rally your intent
and face an impersonal dawn

Rally your intent
and face an impersonal dawn

Rally your intent
and face an impersonal dawn

Stanza Break

Rally your intent
and face an impersonal dawn   # # #

SILENCE ALWAYS RHYMES
(spoken in stammered speech as simile volleyed toward a John Cage composition)

You know
it isn't anything you did
or the way you look... not necessarily
It isn't even that I like you much
as a person, because I don't always
You do some things that aren't kind
they are even insensitive
But... but
when I kiss you
the few times I have kissed you
my soul - o.k. soul is too poetic
but when we kiss
there is a space present
it's large and dark
and I can't go there
carrying baggage
I mean if Jesus could kiss like you
I'd just follow
I'd be religious
because there is a spirit
and that spirit descends
bending trees and crosses
anything that doesn't have the faith
to be moved
And, however briefly
I am in your arms
each moment seems
suspended along filaments of light
I know in the forefront
of your mind, the mind that
has ridden in the decay of my car
the mind that seeks luxury

the spirit crosses even that
and hovers wet and suspicious
The value of it couldn't register there
so, its presence appears more
like a narcotic, an escape
But each time you deny it
it's the cock crowing again
and death comes by degrees
it isn't some isolated event
Pleasure actually increases
our survival - and just look around you
the ones we love all have an albatross
about their necks over this
there is a mood of destruction
when the spirit de-scends
and we don't follow
because there is a painful awareness
of what we don't have
of what is missing from our lives
De-tails start to go awry
people's demands take on this
stark intolerable clarity
and those demands have the weight
of chains pulled taut
from every conceivable direction

I look at your face
and you probably figure
my eyes stop there
but they don't
that would be more like
a transaction
When I hear you speak
the words you choose
can be as
unconscious as a cash register
So, I imagine this poem
echoing through folds of vanity
and words like kiss
getting translated into attachment
or some word that contains
responsibility and irresponsibility
secretly below each s
And I question the demands

of the spirit
Why is it dancing here
It's so inconvenient
it's apparently foolhardy
but that makes my vanity
far larger than your own
So, I try to do as it instructs
and its abstract pressure
cancels all other illusions
the way fire does
leaving only ashes

Your world is all an elaborate device
to support a complex carbon chain
that we breathe the word "human" across
mine is always a mystery
and in it
you have a power
larger even that the appetites
of carbon chains
You actually GLOW
and I do not pretend
to have all that much to offer
really, there are only my eyes
and I have given them to you just now
Avoiding them will not help you
because you feel them without my presence
they seek the lowest level
like water, and lets face it
you're thirsty
The particular ease you felt in my embrace
comes back the way a song rises
and nothing more can be said
The days are numbered
stop pretending you're immortal
take a little time - an hour maybe -
and look back across the years
How many number the days
that you knew that kind of ease
that com-pleteness
The embarrassment of being discovered
found out
and liked anyway
Go ... go ahead add them up
just don't speak the number too loud

See, what I don't think you get
is that I don't find you
any great prize
I would not be here
of my own volition
it's just that we seem to work
and I do not pretend to understand why

Just come a little closer
before we get reduced
like the heat on a pre-fall day
when you suddenly realize
it's missing, and probably not coming back
I seek only repose
large and dark
bathed in that spirit's
de-scent   # # #

THE QUEEN OF CUPS

That absolute idiot
Joanna Rhee
was fighting bulls and locusts
simultaneously
she lived on some property
up Star Route 10
She was the queen of cups
and it's a tale that begins
drinking liquor from paper
and burning a coal fire
dull red
while the last sliver of moon
fell west of Omaha
and there was no sky
after that
The waters from the earth
took that personal
and rose up
leaving us dry
and dreaming about
the taste of each other's blood

Our Conversation pretty much ceased
what with the bulls and the locusts
and three demons appeared
each taking a letter
from my name
and hiding
(thieves that they were)
behind the few remaining trees
those trees were already pissed
and they didn't take well to the demons
so, I always knew
right where the demons were
waiting, maybe 200 yards from the house

I'd laugh real loud
and stand on my head
it seemed to entice the creatures
who'd get curious
as to why
I didn't want my name back
and they'd inch up
filthy and stinking
for a closer look
and I'd glare at them
upside down

Now, Joanna Rhee
was given to a passion
I've never known
but heard plenty of
on nights when the moon
would have been full
if I counted correctly
and the entire house would sing
rising through a hole
where the sky might have been
and I'd sleep with a demon
under each arm
and one at my feet
watching the crystal rattle
in a cabinet from China
and I slipped one time
and looked into that crystal
where I saw a future
that never came to pass
I killed the demons right then and there
and left the property looking
for an entry into a past
west of Omaha
where the future
might still be hanging with the moon
and an ordinary life
spread out on a typewriter
the fool
born from the queen of cups   # # #

ON FRAMING

Humping the centuries
that is history
to me
you love
and hate
consumptively -
but I get romantic
now and again.
Imagine a time
when painting served architecture
the act itself
relegated
to motifs
an adornment
to walls.
These people
said guild
like we do union
were denied
choice
and thought.
Then it was
Van Eyck
I think
who first said
stretcher frame ...
they stick it
on the wall,
decide it needs
a further frame
you know
like a window
suddenly
perspective
becomes visible

to everyone.
Van Eyck
a subjective hero
of Kim's mind -
who really knows
what he was like?
The garden wall
a paradigm
the bastard son
a schedule
the windows
the fences
and borders
a politic
a cause
a careful defense
the firmness
of a rectangle
no matter
how visceral.
It's as if
awareness
needs a lie
to keep
the wall out.
The bliss
of ignorance
as human appetite
a happy
giving up
and then
you get
a Cubist in there
to shake things
fracture
the fun.
The frame now
is visible,
everyone can see it,
perspective goes the way
of walls.

A circle lies
unconsidered
round like a village

13 like the lunar months
or 12 like the sun
it pulls at your shadow
and dances in blood.
Possession
nature takes back
its body
rubs into it
humus and fire.
The skies open
thunder
your lover might
devour you here
and be justified.
The mood
the location
the direction
circle
pull you unwittingly
across the seasons
wear your pride
into submission
fling body to rock
lift you on breezes
massage each of your senses
course evenly through each orifice
turning first to liquid
then air.
The scale
of green alone
cradles you
calm
races you
fluid as panther
down a path
unseen.
The spinning
the circle
the circle
that calls
in the eyes
of your ancestor,
begs you to explain
holds council so gentle
it could butterfly.

Stanza Break

There is I should think
a basic shape to things.
A low, unintelligible
whisper
that bends
words into form
and so too
the creatures
that inhabit them.   ###

INLOUD

IN BEGINNING

A crow calls
in a place where
broken cylinders of time
coalesce   ###

ON SOIL COMPOSITION

The soil where we stand
is half air
it is alive with
countless organisms
there are large pores
small pores
it is a vast area
of decay in two directions
the plants from above
that fall to rest
the parent stone
from below
that breaks up
and mixes fractionally smaller
into solution with the quicker kindoms
It is a zone of transmutation
bursting
collapsing
into itself
grinding, rubbing together
compacting
ripping open into furrows
Our seeds drop along it
Our bodies fall onto it
Each body given its own voice
speaking in the key
of its parent material
the particular stone
that lies unseen below
We are the dreams of those stones
gone out for a walk
They speak the way
cities speak
in large codes
in sets of possibilities

It pays to know
something of the stone
you were born from
something of the stone
you have moved to
I am writing atop
limestone
I was born from
quartz and flint
I flee when I am able
to jasper, basalt, granite
and always the quartz
of my childhood
made round
by the slurry of centuries
It helps to know
the speed of stones
in the delirium of air
where the consequence of a storm
alters nothing.

It is a great wisdom
of plants
to reach two ways -
I suppose our teeth
should know this   # # #

AT ASH SKIN BREAKS

and the bet was -
I couldn't roll
the parrot legs
of summer
skinny
through Ash Skin Breaks
toward that other shore
and have them chant
sense into the dull ache
we figured for desire
all the while
counting backwards
from one hundred
the lesser mistakes
that etched as acid
among copper plates
the lines of a world
barely discussed
and left unremembered
in the actions and dust
of travelers passing
in odd hours
the unfamiliar cars
of stories
we would gladly
fuck to death
for tobacco
left to flower
and a quick peek
beneath a veil
left hanging awkward
against the brink   # # #

OLD WOMAN'S BROOM

There is a glorious poverty
that carves into the calendar
the way unpublished notes
between lovers might
mention the price of bread
in a given year, or
an urgent declaration of emotion
that wrinkles cotton and material
against an ordinary noon
and cloudless sky

In the hard light
chisel of days
counted in paychecks
and twelve nouns
whose true meanings
have been stripped
like the racks of
some clever business failure
in an out-of-the-way mall ...
We see the old woman's broom
and hear it against the porch
SWEEPING   SWEEPING
We count our pop bottles
and save the wine corks
We join hands in small bands
and turn circles
through an abstraction
of our parents brand of reason
spinning - lifting - spinning - dropping
along that curtain in front of the moon
Days - little darlin' - these ARE the days

I burn along your eyelids
then shoot the entablature

---

of the storefronts
I take a bath on your lips
that haven't a bitter complaint
left in them
The banknotes here are
printed on air and dreams
and we spend them freely
in the cafes and shops
whose walls are conversations
The rich earth of your desires
anchors me, sprouts me
an inverted tree
who has opted against movement
in favor of connection
and out of necessity reinvents
the future in ten thousand
possibilities of green ...
We see the old woman's broom
and hear it against the porch
SWEEPING   SWEEPING   # # #

CABINETS

This woman said
"I opened up
my cabinets
and there was every simple
thing
I ever wanted."
The butterflies
are now leaves
the earth quite wet -
It smells relaxing
like a dream
some small part of me
is empty and vacant
I let it rise
to join its counterpart
noticing that when
they meet
their scales are equal
A man falling
leaves
against a course
butterflies once took
past the window
of a dreamer
in a room with books ...
The magic dances
done in empty spaces
a common character
(cross referenced)
easy like a laugh
begged to become
entire afternoons
falling
flitting
turning

around
spaces merging
The brittle snap
away from branch
the intoxicated fall
into flower
picture
page
image
please
stay

butterfly over
leaves falling
every simple thing
I ever wanted
open   # # #

DETROIT

This bitter cold cat
cuts through a tire track
in eight inches of snow.
He looks back
and sums me up
quicker than a calculator
with two single digits ...

these cold, concise steps
into meaning.   ###

CHIVE POD CITY

This text is collapsing
Cities shaped like seed pods
drier than October
heavy too
phloem no longer rising
in the stem
the root seems distant
absurdly connected
given wind
on skinny extremities
The fall to earth
The call of roots
that must now be mimicked
reconstructed
by a deep body knowing

No inventory is ever accurate
this text is collapsing
It is all
chance
and soil
and rainfall
Nature blasts
the location a given
going forth
memory expressed in action
in going
not recalled
because
no inventory is ever accurate

this text is collapsing   # # #

RURAL AS EVERYWHERE

Men of visions
and English letters
tear cows in half
and do their chores
mad about the women
they almost knew

This we call home
the sharply divided ground
dictating compact crops
along a fence row

Yours and mine
us and them
a common interest
of mornings
abstractly filtered
through surveyors tools
where each ignored
song bird
increases our debt load
where foreclosure
is a birth right
where a flaming door
opens anyway ...
it opens on an afternoon
average as any
and the only thing
that fits through it
is the fleeting recall
of a lover's face
bathed in some innocent sleep
where words were not spoken
and someone left unseen   # # #

WATERFALL

The ceaseless giving
of the waterfall;
itself unto the rocks -
and it takes a stone
to accept such abundance
transported as it were
to the delicacy of desert
an echo
of unknown origin
spoken away
from each flat plane
The species
dividing through cultivar
shimmers in the gases
of breath
a remembered molecule
rediscovered along
an unfamiliar tongue
inserted more urgent than air
pressing through concrete
and other delusions
of solidity ... permanence
rendered in moonlight
the more affordable garment
of the second hand store
that once discarded
reveals dawn again
for the first time
The gods are immortal
because they are newborn
in each second
and "ancient" is a lie
to explain what happened
when we went out for a walk   # # #

OBTECT ARMS

The dry, random sound of
a pine cone dropping
in an acre of uncut wood.

The arms of the obtect
seen against the clarity
of sky.

The soil
The blood
The season of language -
speaking winds.
The archaic idea of quality.
The genuine kindness of a face
that asks for nothing
and maintains its distance
as the sun reflects
the same verb
...twice.   ###

BACK FROM LAKE SUPERIOR (FORGIVE ME)

If the sky were not dynamic
and remained a constant gray
If the wind chime had not been invented ...
I could not burn this candle
as I am now
looking at rocks collected
along a stretch of beach
a beach respirating,
breathing its first breath -
a perpetual series of first breaths
knowing neither the command
of its origin
nor the direction
of its path
knowing only
a breath
a repetition
a success
a void
It is filling
ceaselessly
all that it is
It is distinct
and narrow
and self aware
for a breath
for every breath
for the total number of breaths
and returns
where I can not see it

A great leaping out of nothing
come these breathing things
knowing narrowly
what silence
has conceded   # # #

RURAL SUMMER

A hundred days
without benefit of magic
each moment solid
and long as the
four o'clock shadows
of summer.
The chair rocks
on the porch
unaided by breeze
or senility ...
the street is empty.   ###

1974 BELMONT

In the slurry near Grand Maris
jasper spins against basalt
quartz and
granite

I'm tappin' my toes
smoking
the neighborhood bat
is doing erratic circles
over the lawn
when this thought breaks
against the porch
and the sound of Lake Superior
comes rushing back -
it is a bit like dawn
spreading April open
for the first time

Here is to the holes jasper carves in basalt
Here is to thunder
and six citronella candles bought on sale
Summer is running nigh on empty
My God where does it all go?
Your voice rented
a car at the airport,
I heard it
The momentum
our habits take on
going forever out
on paths of least resistance
and you think like basalt
about breaking down
one smooth holes worth
of letting go
into the chaos of perception

---

that ocean
of limitless black light
propping all these images up
on a night as fine as this
when eighty percent of your block
is watching commercial television ...
the world feels a bit neglected
and sound becomes an odd movement
in the corner of the garden
with no meaning
to prove its
existence
the night half drunk
and hungry   # # #

STORIES

The grackle on the maple
and the mouse in the cupboards
both tell a storm
through the peninsula
different   ###

"His imagination is a theater in ruins, a baleful perch for parrots and crows."

Andre Breton
A LETTER TO SEERS

WHERE DIFFERENCES LIE

I am given to tremendous gardens
and I am at my garden
not as a metaphor
not as a place you could
ever read about

The birds have never begged
the question of its originality as an idea
yet, they come to drink
I've tried to convince them
to teach me to fly -
figuring I'd save on plane fare
to an afternoon someplace
where emotion didn't have
the constitution of quick silver ...
but the birds are nothing more
than messengers
and pay little attention
to my demands

Night after night
when I'm through pulling weeds
I try to spell the word
continuity
so perfectly
with such

unbending intent
that it could form seeds
for these birds
and I
They
I know
would then cease to fly
but there again is my dilemma
explaining
as I often try
"the imagination of reference"

Look
there below every grand call
to your metaphoric arms
is a scene just like mine
without a hell of alot of drama
just tea well chosen
and company sometimes   # # #

A MAP

Left = perception engaged
in microcosm

Right = perception engaged
in macrocosm

Where I is located:
PAST<<<<<<<<<<<<<<<<<<<<<<<<<<<<PRESENT>>>>>>>>>>>>>>>>>>>>>>>>FUTURE

What I is:
HISTORY<<<<<<<<<<<<<<<<<<<<<<<<<<STORY>>>>>>>>>>>>>>>>>>>>>>>>>DREAMS

How I is made:
REASON <<<<<<<<<<<<<<<<<<<<<<<<ISNESS>>>>>>>>>>>>>>>>>>>>>>>>POSSIBILITIES

^-CONCERN{ }REPOSE-^

giving

< HUNTING   (having)   CULTIVATING >

taking

Active - Passive
^-ENERGY-^
# # #

RIDGEWAY PRESS BOOKS
Since 1974

1990 *The Violence of Potatoes,*
Faye Kicknosway
snakecrossing,
Lolita Hernandez
Blood M. Ther.
Lorene Erikson
Salad in August.
Stella L. Crews
Conformities,
Laurence W. Thomas
1991 *Pierced by Sound.*
Lawrence Pike
Home Before Light.
Cheri Fein
(US)
Michael Castro
Bearing Witness.
Bob Hicok
The Lingo of Beer.
Rudy Baron
A Passionate Distance,
Joan Gartland
Gittin Down:
An Anthology of Prison Writings
The Cursive World.
Marc J. Sheenan
Deliver Me,
M. L. Liebler
Labor Pains.
Edited by Leon Chamberlain
1992 *Stations of the Cross.*
John R. Reed
A Modern Fairy Tale: The Baba Yaga Poems,
Linda Nemec Foster
Listen To Me,
Faye Kicknosway
The Vision of Words: Michigan Poets,
Edited by M. L. Liebler
Photographs by John Sobczak
Hacking It,
Jim Daniels
On A Good Day,
Gay Rubin
de KANSAS a CALIFAS & back to CHICAGO,
Carlos Cortez
Mystical,
Dalmation
Deer Crossing/Leap Years Away,
William Boyer
Fragile Visions,
Josef Bastian
Raking the Gravel & Other Poems,
Ben Bohnhorst
Macro-Harmonic Music Manuscript Workbook,
Faruq Z. Bey
1993 *Hunger And Other Poems,*
Geoffrey Jacques
Mysterious Coleslaw,
Pamela Miller
Still Life With Conversation,
Rebecca Emlinger Roberts

1993 *The Short Life of The 5 Minute Dancer,*
Barry Wallenstein
Water Music,
Robert Haight
The Hollow Moon,
Edited by M. L. Liebler
Dream of The Black Wolf,
Keith Taylor
1994 *Images Cadiennes (Cajun Images)*
Beverly Matherne
Palimpsest,
Anne Hutchinson
Victrola,
Danny Rendleman
Pierced By Sound,
Lawrence Pike (Second Printing)
No Sporting Chance,
K.C. Washington
The Hollow Moon
Edited by M. L. Liebler
The Red Eye Incident,
A Special Community Writing Project
A Service On The Sufficiency of Feeding Finches,
Ben Bohnhorst
Bloodline Poems,
.Del Corey
1995 *Convalescence and Other Poems,*
Tyrone Williams (Third Printing)
Great Lake,
John R. Reed
Descent From The Cross,
Ben Bohnhorst
Memory Bags,
Thom Jurek
Bye Bye DDR,
Eugene Chadbourne
Zodiac Arrest,
Rochelle Ratner
The Middle West,
Danny Rendleman
Time Is Not Linear,
Cindi St. Germain
Perfume And Tears,
Ben Bohnhorst
1996 *Peacocks & Beans,*
Valerie Tekavec
Letters to Che
Melba Joyce Boyd
I Want My Body Back
Ron Allen
Fweivel: The Day Will Come
Frazier Russell
Abstract Cores,
Kim Webb

*Out of Print